GW00888844

THE STATION
THE CROSS
IN JERUSALEM

PRAYERS OF
ST. ALPHONSUS LIGUORI

Edited by G.S.P. Freeman - Grenville

Photography by Philip Giggle

Preface by the Right Reverend
Augustine Harris
Bishop of Middlesbrough

EAST-WEST PUBLICATIONS
LONDON AND THE HAGUE

PREFACE

This presentation of the Stations of the Cross by Dr. Freeman-Grenville is most opportune. In effect, the Stations of the Cross are telling us that religion is not a collection of dogmatic formulae, but the bringing together of people on their pilgrimage to God. For the Christian it is the person of Jesus Christ who gathers and leads the human race and the way he takes us is the Way of the Cross.

This is a paradox. We do not expect to find the happiness of God at the end of a trail of sufferings, but this is precisely the message of the Stations of the Cross. We must strain and suffer before we achieve serenity.

The paradox of pain is a mystery. Christ does not explain the mystery – he goes through it, publicly and in agony. He then invites us to follow.

Christ, Calvary and the Cross – these are not just sad echoes of history. Today we are called to take up our present cross and follow. This presentation of the Stations of the Cross by Dr Freeman-Grenville is telling us that the Way of the Cross is for the one who follows Christ now. The original Way of the Cross is still there physically. The 20th Century pilgrim walks along it. Dr Freeman-Grenville has transplanted archaeology and history so that they may live on in 20th Century devotion. We need this reassurance that the Way of the Cross is still the way to resurrection and the glory of God.

†Augustine Harris,
Bishop of Middlesbrough

INTRODUCTION

The Stations of the Cross in Jerusalem commemorate fourteen incidents in the Passion of Our Lord Jesus Christ at places between the Praetorium and the Holy Sepulchre. Some of these are based on the Gospels, others on tradition. There are two schools of thought among scholars about the actual place of Jesus' trial and route to Calvary. The route followed in the Procession in Jerusalem at 3 p.m. each Friday, and solemnly on Good Friday, led by the Franciscans, is hallowed by many centuries of piety.

Already in the life-time of Eusebius (AD 260-340), historian and Bishop of Caesarea, bishops and pilgrims flocked to Jerusalem. The Emperor Constantine the Great made the Holy Places in Jerusalem the focal centre of Christendom by building, in 326-36, Basilicas of the Resurrection (*Anastasis*) and of the Cross, now both rebuilt and enclosed in the mainly Crusader Church of the Holy Sepulchre.

Pilgrims have used a number of routes along what was known as the Holy Way, and now the Via Dolorosa, since the thirteenth century, when the Stations of the Cross became a popular devotion. The number of Stations, or halts of the Procession for prayers, has also varied from time to time. Some changes have been due to structural changes in the town plan of Jerusalem. From the thirteenth century onwards, following the lead of the Franciscans, the devotion of the Way of the Cross, or the Stations of the Cross, spread all over Europe. Today no Catholic Church of the Latin rite is without representations of the Stations.

There are no prescribed prayers for this devotion. When they are made in common, it is recommended to sing a verse of the *Stabat Mater* between each Station, or some other hymn; and to recite an act of contrition, the Our Father and the Hail Mary, and to pray for the Pope's intention. Thus various forms of public prayers have been composed. Those printed here are those of St Alphonsus Liguori (1696-1787), the form most widely used in England.

Sheriff Hutton, York.   G.S.P.F.-G.

Courtyard of el-Omariyeh College

Jesus' condemnation to death by Pontius Pilate is commemorated in el-Omariyeh College courtyard, the site of the Praetorium (St John 18.28-19.16). In its inner hall the soldiers scourged Jesus, crowned him with thorns and mocked him. The trial was outside in the paved courtyard (Greek: Lithostrotos, *Hebrew* Gabbatha).

Prayer before the Altar

O Jesus Christ, my Lord, with what great love didst thou pass over the painful road which led thee to death; and I, how often have I abandoned thee! But now I love thee with my whole soul, and because I love thee I am sincerely sorry for having offended thee. My Jesus, pardon me, and permit me to accompany thee in this journey. Thou art going to die for love of me, and it is my wish also, my dearest Redeemer, to die for love of thee. My Jesus, in thy love I wish to live. In thy love I wish to die.

THE FIRST STATION

*

JESUS IS CONDEMNED TO DEATH

V. We adore thee, O Christ, and praise thee
R. Because by thy holy Cross thou hast redeemed the world.

Consider how Jesus, after having been scourged and crowned with thorns, was unjustly condemned by Pilate to die on the Cross.

My loving Jesus, it was not Pilate; no, it was my sins that condemned thee to die. I beseech thee, by the merits of this sorrowful journey, to assist my soul in her journey towards eternity.

I love thee, Jesus, my love, above all things; I repent with my whole heart of having offended thee. Never permit me to separate myself from thee again. Grant that I may love thee always; and then do with me what thou wilt.

Our Father.   Hail Mary.   Glory be to the Father.

At the Cross her station keeping
Stood the mournful Mother weeping,
Close to Jesus at the last.

Outside the Lithostrotos

Jesus' receiving the Cross is commemorated in the street outside the Lithostrotos. Part still retains paving contemporary with Jesus. (We actually tread on stones on which he trod.) Visible thereon are marks made by games played by Roman soldiers, possibly during Jesus' trial. One game, Basilinda, mocked a man as king.

THE SECOND STATION

*

JESUS RECEIVES HIS CROSS

V.   We adore thee, O Christ, and praise thee
R.   Because by thy holy Cross thou hast redeemed the
     world.

*Consider how Jesus, in making this journey with the
Cross on his shoulders, thought of us, and offered for us
to his Father the death he was about to undergo.*

My most beloved Jesus! I embrace all the tribulations thou
hast destined for me until death. I beseech thee, by the
merits of the pain thou didst suffer in carrying thy Cross, to
give me the necessary help to carry mine with perfect
patience and resignation.

I love thee, Jesus, my love, above all things; I repent with
my whole heart of having offended thee. Never permit me
to separate myself from thee again. Grant that I may love
thee always; and then do with me what thou wilt.

Our Father.   Hail Mary.   Glory be to the Father.

> Through her heart his sorrow sharing,
> All his bitter anguish bearing,
> Now at length the sword had passed.

Entrance to the Polish chapel

The Third Station, at the corner of the street, is not mentioned in the Gospels. The tradition of Jesus' first fall is ancient, and a little later the Roman soldiers made an African, Simon of Cyrene (in Libya) shoulder the Cross. The chapel was renovated in 1947-8 by offerings from the Polish Army in Palestine.

THE THIRD STATION

*

JESUS FALLS UNDER HIS CROSS FOR THE FIRST TIME

V.   We adore thee, O Christ, and praise thee
R.   Because by thy holy Cross thou hast redeemed the world.

Consider this first fall of Jesus under his Cross. His flesh was torn by the scourges, his head was crowned with thorns; he had lost a great quantity of blood. So weakened he could hardly walk, he yet had to carry this great load upon his shoulders. The soldiers struck him rudely, and he fell several times.

My Jesus, it is the weight, not of the Cross, but of my sins, which has made thee suffer so much pain. By the merits of this first fall, deliver me from the misfortune of falling into mortal sin.

I love thee, Jesus, my love, above all things; I repent with my whole heart of having offended thee. Never permit me to separate myself from thee again. Grant that I may love thee always; and then do with me what thou wilt.

Our Father.   Hail Mary.   Glory be to the Father.

Oh, how sad and sore distressed
Was that Mother highly blessed
Of the sole-begotten one!

Entrance of the Church of Our Lady of the Spasm

The Fourth Station is made outside the Armenian Catholic Church of Our Lady of the Spasm. In the crypt, at ancient street level, is a mosaic, probably belonging to the former Church of St Sophia, and earlier than the seventh century, which is believed to mark the place where Jesus met his Mother.

THE FOURTH STATION

*

JESUS MEETS HIS AFFLICTED MOTHER

V.   We adore thee, O Christ, and praise thee
R.   Because by thy holy Cross thou hast redeemed the
     world.

*Consider the meeting of the Son and the Mother, which
took place on this journey. Their looks became like so
many arrows to wound those hearts which loved each
other so tenderly.*

My sweet Jesus, by the sorrow thou didst experience in this
meeting, grant me the grace of a devoted love for thy Holy
Mother. And thou, my Queen, who wast overwhelmed
with sorrow, obtain for me a continual and tender remem-
brance of the Passion of thy Son.

   I love thee, Jesus, my love, above all things; I repent with
my whole heart of having offended thee. Never permit me
to separate myself from thee again. Grant that I may love
thee always; and then do with me what thou wilt.

Our Father.   Hail Mary.   Glory be to the Father.

          Christ above in torments hangs;
          She beneath beholds the pangs
          Of her dying glorious Son.

Entrance of the Oratory of St. Simon of Cyrene

The Fifth Station is the first in the Via Dolorosa properly so called. Here a stranger from Cyrene, a Libyan, Simon, was made to help Jesus carry his Cross. Scripture only mentions him as the father of Alexander and Rufus. Near here the Franciscans had their first house in 1229-44.

THE FIFTH STATION

*

SIMON OF CYRENE HELPS JESUS CARRY HIS CROSS

V.   We adore thee, O Christ, and praise thee
R.   Because by thy holy Cross thou hast redeemed the world.

Consider how his cruel tormentors, seeing Jesus was on the point of expiring, and fearing he would die on the way, whereas they wished him to die the shameful death of the Cross, constrained Simon of Cyrene to carry the Cross behind our Lord.

My most beloved Jesus, by thy grace I will not refuse to carry the Cross; I accept it, I embrace it. I accept in particular the death thou hast destined for me, with all the pains which may accompany it; I unite it to thy death, I offer it to thee. Thou hast died for love of me; I will die for love of thee. Help me by thy grace.

I love thee, Jesus, my love, above all things; I repent with my whole heart of having offended thee. Never permit me to separate myself from thee again. Grant that I may love thee always; and then do with me what thou wilt.

Our Father.   Hail Mary.   Glory be to the Father.

Is there one who would not weep,
Whelmed in miseries so deep
Christ's dear Mother to behold?

Interior of Chapel of St. Veronica

Eighty yards after the Fifth Station a column inserted in a wall marks the house of a Jerusalem lady named Veronica in which now is the Chapel of St. Veronica. She is believed to have wiped Jesus' face with a handkerchief as he passed by; when she withdrew it, his features were said to have been imprinted upon it.

The Sixth Station

*

Veronica Wipes the Face of Jesus

V.   We adore thee, O Christ, and praise thee
R.   Because by thy holy Cross thou hast redeemed the
world.

*Consider how the holy woman named Veronica, seeing
Jesus so ill-used, and bathed in sweat and blood, wiped
his face with a towel, on which was left the impression of
his holy countenance.*

My most beloved Jesus! Thy face was beautiful before, but
in this journey it has lost all its beauty, and wounds and
blood have disfigured it. Alas! my soul also was once
beautiful, when it received thy grace in baptism; but I have
disfigured it by my sins; thou alone, my Redeemer, canst
restore it to its former beauty. Do this by thy Passion, O
Jesus!

I love thee, Jesus, my love, above all things; I repent with
my whole heart of having offended thee. Never permit me
to separate myself from thee again. Grant that I may love
thee always; and then do with me what thou wilt.

Our Father.   Hail Mary.   Glory be to the Father.

Can the human heart refrain
From partaking in her pain,
In that Mother's pain untold?

Chapels of the Second Fall of Jesus

The Via Dolorosa now rises sharply up a hill. Once there was a gate here, called the Gate of Judgement, where sentences of death were posted up. This, according to tradition, was too much for Jesus' spent strength. He fell again. There are two Franciscan chapels here, one above the other.

THE SEVENTH STATION

*

JESUS FALLS THE SECOND TIME

V.   We adore thee, O Christ, and praise thee
R.   Because by thy holy Cross thou hast redeemed the
world.

*Consider the second fall of Jesus under the Cross, a fall
which renews the pain of all the wounds in his head and
members.*

My Jesus, how many times hast thou pardoned me, and
how many times have I fallen again, and begun to offend
thee. By the merits of this second fall, give me the help
necessary to persevere in thy grace until death. Grant that
in all temptations which assail me I may always commend
myself to thee.

I love thee, Jesus, my love, above all things; I repent with
my whole heart of having offended thee. Never permit me
to separate myself from thee again. Grant that I may love
thee always; and then do with me what thou wilt.

Our Father.   Hail Mary.   Glory be to the Father.

Bruised, derided, cursed, defiled,
She beheld her tender Child
All with bloody scourges rent.

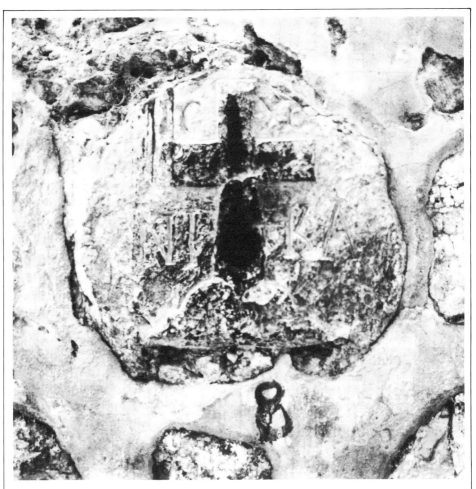

Inscription on the wall of the Greek convent

The Eighth Station is marked by a Latin Cross and the Greek words – IC XP / NIKA (Jesus Christ conquers!). Here Jesus was met by a crowd of weeping women. He implored them to think, not of himself, but of their children – and of their own sins.

THE EIGHTH STATION

*

JESUS SPEAKS TO THE WOMEN OF JERUSALEM

V.   We adore thee, O Christ, and praise thee
R.   Because by thy holy Cross thou hast redeemed the
     world.

Consider how these women wept with compassion at seeing Jesus in such a pitiable state, streaming with blood as he walked along. 'Daughters of Jerusalem,' said he, 'weep not for me, but for yourselves and for your children.'

My Jesus, laden with sorrows! I weep for the offences I have committed against thee because of the pains they have deserved, and still more because of the displeasure they have caused thee, who hast loved me so much. It is thy love more than the fear of hell which causes me to weep for my sins.

   I love thee, Jesus, my love, above all things; I repent with my whole heart of having offended thee. Never permit me to separate myself from thee again. Grant that I may love thee always; and then do with me what thou wilt.

Our Father.   Hail Mary.   Glory be to the Father.

For the sins of his own nation
Saw him hang in desolation
Till his spirit forth he sent.

Pillar outside Coptic Patriarchate

Although a long detour is needed to reach Calvary through the Church of the Holy Sepulchre, we are now very close to the top of the hill. Here, according to tradition, Jesus fell to the ground for the third time. The place is marked by a pillar set in a doorway.

THE NINTH STATION

*

JESUS FALLS THE THIRD TIME

V.   We adore thee, O Christ, and praise thee
R.   Because by thy holy Cross thou hast redeemed the
world.

*Consider the third fall of Jesus Christ. His weakness was
extreme, and the cruelty of his executioners excessive,
who tried to hasten his steps when he could scarcely
move.*

My outraged Jesus, by the merits of the weakness thou
didst suffer in going to Calvary, give me strength to
conquer all human respect, and my wicked passions, which
have led me to despise thy friendship.

I love thee, Jesus, my love, above all things; I repent with
my whole heart of having offended thee. Never permit me
to separate myself from thee again. Grant that I may love
thee always; and then do with me what thou wilt.

Our Father.   Hail Mary.   Glory be to the Father.

O thou Mother! Fount of love!
Touch my spirit from above.
Make my heart with thine accord.

Calvary – right hand nave

Fourteen steps lead to the top of Calvary, which is wholly enclosed today in the Church of the Holy Sepulchre. It was once a separate shrine, with two naves. Tradition places where the soldiers stripped Jesus of his clothes in the right hand nave as one enters. The steps up to it are steep, and must always have been difficult. This Station, together with the whole southern nave, belongs to the Franciscans. The Station is marked by a geometric pattern on the floor.

THE TENTH STATION

*

JESUS IS STRIPPED OF HIS GARMENTS

V. We adore thee, O Christ, and praise thee
R. Because by thy holy Cross thou hast redeemed the
world.

*Consider the violence with which Jesus was stripped by
the executioners. His inner garments adhered to his torn
flesh, and they dragged them off so roughly that the skin
came with them. Feel compassion for your Saviour so
cruelly treated.*

My most innocent Jesus! By the merits of the torment thou
hast felt, help me to strip myself of all affection to things of
earth, that I may place all my love in thee, who art so
worthy of my love.

I love thee, Jesus, my love, above all things; I repent with
my whole heart of having offended thee. Never permit me
to separate myself from thee again. Grant that I may love
thee always; and then do with me what thou wilt.

Our Father.   Hail Mary.   Glory be to the Father.

Make me feel as thou hast felt;
Make my soul to glow and melt
With the love of Christ my Lord.

Altar of the Nailing to the Cross

The Latin altar on the right hand side of the nave of Calvary marks the place where Jesus is believed to have been nailed to the Cross. Ropes would also have been necessary to prevent the hands and feet from slipping away from the nails. The mosaic depicting the Crucifixion was put here by the Franciscans in 1937. The altar dates from 1558.

THE ELEVENTH STATION

*

JESUS IS NAILED TO THE CROSS

V. We adore thee, O Christ, and praise thee
R. Because by thy holy Cross thou hast redeemed the
world.

*Consider how Jesus, having been placed upon the Cross,
extended his hands, and offered to his eternal Father
the sacrifice of his life for our salvation. Those barbarians
fastened him with nails, and then, securing the Cross,
allowed him to die with anguish on this infamous gibbet.*

My Jesus, loaded with contempt, nail my heart to thy feet,
that it may ever remain there, to love thee, and never more
to leave thee.

I love thee, Jesus, my love, above all things; I repent with
my whole heart of having offended thee. Never permit me
to separate myself from thee again. Grant that I may love
thee always; and then do with me what thou wilt.

Our Father.   Hail Mary.   Glory be to the Father.

Holy Mother! pierce me through;
In my heart each wound renew
Of my Saviour crucified.

Calvary – where the Cross stood

Coming into the left hand side of the nave, the Greek altar marks the place of the Crucifixion. Underneath it in the middle is a silver disc, with a hole marking where the Cross stood. On either side of it black marble discs mark the places of the crosses of the two thieves.

THE TWELFTH STATION

*

JESUS DIES ON THE CROSS

V.   We adore thee, O Christ, and praise thee
R.   Because by thy holy Cross thou hast redeemed the
world.

*Consider how Jesus, being consumed with anguish after
three hours' agony on the Cross, abandoned himself to
the weight of his body, bowed his head and died.*

O my dying Jesus! I kiss devoutly the Cross on which thou
didst die for love of me. I have merited by my sins to die a
miserable death, but thy death is my hope. By the merits of
thy death, give me grace to die embracing thy feet, and
burning with love for thee. I commit my soul into thy
hands.

I love thee, Jesus, my love, above all things; I repent with
my whole heart of having offended thee. Never permit me
to separate myself from thee again. Grant that I may love
thee always; and then do with me what thou wilt.

Our Father.   Hail Mary.   Glory be to the Father.

Let me share with him his pain,
Who for all my sins was slain,
Who for me in torments died.

Calvary – where Our Lady stood

Between the Eleventh and Twelfth Stations is the Latin Altar of Stabat Mater, with a seventeenth century bust of Our Lady of Sorrows, covered with votive offerings of jewels and gold. Here Our Lady stood while her Son was dying; and here his dead body was given into her arms.

THE THIRTEENTH STATION

*

JESUS IS TAKEN DOWN FROM THE CROSS

V.   We adore thee, O Christ, and praise thee

R.   Because by thy holy Cross thou hast redeemed the world.

Consider how, after our Lord had expired, two of his disciples, Joseph and Nicodemus, took him down from the Cross, and placed him in the arms of his afflicted Mother, who received him with unutterable tenderness and pressed him to her bosom.

O Mother of Sorrow, for the love of this Son, accept me for thy servant, and pray for me. And thou, my Redeemer, since thou hast died for me, permit me to love thee; for I wish but thee, and nothing more.

I love thee, Jesus, my love, above all things; I repent with my whole heart of having offended thee. Never permit me to separate myself from thee again. Grant that I may love thee always; and then do with me what thou wilt.

Our Father.   Hail Mary.   Glory be to the Father.

Let me mingle tears with thee,
Mourning him who mourn'd for me,
All the days that I may live.

The Holy Sepulchre

Jesus' Sepulchre was of traditional Jewish type. An outer chamber led to an inner room, closed by a rolling stone. In 326 the Emperor Constantine the Great removed all but the slab where Jesus' body had been laid, building a shrine round it. The present shrine dates from 1808, its predecessor having been burnt down. A low, narrow opening leads to the Holy Sepulchre, which is covered with a white marble slab. Behind the inner room is a small Coptic chapel in which the actual rock of the Holy Sepulchre can be seen and touched.

The Fourteenth Station

*

Jesus is Laid in the Sepulchre

V. We adore thee, O Christ, and praise thee
R. Because by thy holy Cross thou hast redeemed the
world.

*Consider how the disciples, accompanied by his holy
Mother, carried the body of Jesus to bury it. They closed
the tomb, and all came sorrowfully away.*

My buried Jesus! I kiss the stone that encloses thee. But
thou didst rise again the third day. I beseech thee, by thy
resurrection, to make me rise in glory with thee at the last
day, to be always united with thee in heaven, to praise
thee and love thee for ever.

I love thee, Jesus, my love, above all things; I repent with
my whole heart of having offended thee. Never permit me
to separate myself from thee again. Grant that I may love
thee always; and then do with me what thou wilt.

Our Father.   Hail Mary.   Glory be to the Father.

> By the Cross with thee to stay,
> There with thee to weep and pray,
> Is all I ask of thee to give.

*

An *Our Father, Hail Mary* and *Glory be to the Father* is now
said for the intention of our Holy Father the Pope.

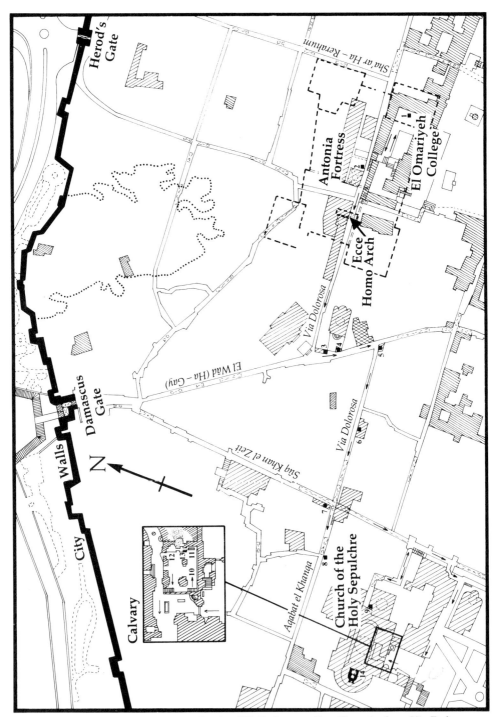

Herod's Gate

Antonia Fortress

El Omariyeh College

Ecce Homo Arch

Sha'ar Ha – Peraḥim

Via Dolorosa

El Wad (Ha – Gay)

Damascus Gate

Sūq Khan el Zeit

N

Via Dolorosa

City Walls

Calvary

Aqabat el Khanqa

Church of the Holy Sepulchre